Michael Nyman

Where the City's Ceaseless Crowds
for Trumpet and Piano

Chester Music

Composer's Note

The title comes from Walt Whitman's poem 'Mannahatta' which was the basis for 'Manhatta' [sic], an experimental film directed by Paul Strand and Charles Sheeler in 1920 and for which Michael Nyman wrote a soundtrack in 2003.

The piece should be played very 'lightly' and the quaver at the end of phrases should be 'lifted' each time.

Duration: c. 2 minutes

Chester Music

part of The Music Sales Group
14–15 Berners Street,
London W1T 3LJ, UK.

Exclusive distributors:
Music Sales Distribution Centre,
Newmarket Road,
Bury St Edmunds,
Suffolk IP33 3YB, UK.

CH81092

www.musicsalesclassical.com

WHERE THE CITY'S CEASELESS CROWDS

Michael Nyman
(2012)

Michael Nyman

Where the City's Ceaseless Crowds

for Trumpet and Piano

(2012)

Chester Music

WHERE THE CITY'S CEASELESS CROWDS

Trumpet in B♭

Michael Nyman
(2012)

più f

cresc. al fine

senza rall.

senza rall.